2024 CICADA PHENOMENON: A GUIDE TO WITNESSING NATURE'S SPECTACLE

TRENDS WITH D'ARCY

THIS BOOK BLONGS TO :

____

TABLE OF CONTENTS

INTRODUCTION

Welcome to an extraordinary journey into the heart of one of nature's most fascinating phenomena—the great cicada emergence of 2024 in the USA. This event, which occurs with clockwork precision every 13 to 17 years, transforms the landscape into a buzzing symphony of life, showcasing the incredible resilience and intricate life cycle of these remarkable insects.

Cicadas are more than just a natural curiosity; they play a vital role in our ecosystem, contributing to nutrient cycling, providing food for predators, and even helping to aerate the soil. Their periodic emergence, marked by the synchronized appearance of millions of insects, offers a unique opportunity to witness nature's complexity and marvel at its wonders.

In "Cicada Invasion 2024: Nature's Hidden Marvels Unveiled," we delve into the world of cicadas, exploring their life cycle, ecological significance, and the unique characteristics of the 2024 emergence. This year promises to be a spectacular display, with cicadas emerging en masse across various regions of the United States, captivating both scientists and the public alike.

The Fascination of Cicadas:
Cicadas have intrigued humans for centuries, featuring prominently in folklore, art, and literature. Their distinctive call, which can reach up to 100 decibels, is a familiar soundtrack to the summer months. But beyond their audible presence, cicadas embody the mysteries of nature—spending the majority of their lives underground only to emerge for a brief, dramatic finale.

Why 2024 is Special:
The 2024 emergence is particularly significant due to the sheer number of cicadas expected and the widespread geographical impact. This event offers a rare chance to study cicadas on a large scale, providing valuable insights into their behaviors, adaptations, and interactions with the environment. It also presents an unparalleled opportunity for communities to engage with and appreciate the natural world.

Our Journey Together:
Throughout this book, we will explore the life stages of cicadas, from eggs to nymphs to adults, and understand their ecological roles. We'll also delve into human experiences and reactions to cicada emergences, providing a comprehensive view of how these insects influence and interact with our world. Each chapter is designed to be informative and engaging, blending scientific facts with captivating anecdotes and visual elements.

Embrace the Buzz:

 As you turn the pages, prepare to be amazed by the intricate details of cicada life and the grand spectacle of their emergence. Whether you are a nature enthusiast, a curious learner, or someone experiencing a cicada emergence for the first time, this book aims to enrich your understanding and appreciation of these incredible insects.

Join us as we uncover the marvels of the 2024 cicada invasion and celebrate the beauty and complexity of nature's hidden wonders.

CHAPTER 1: UNDERSTANDING THE LIFE CYCLE OF CICADAS

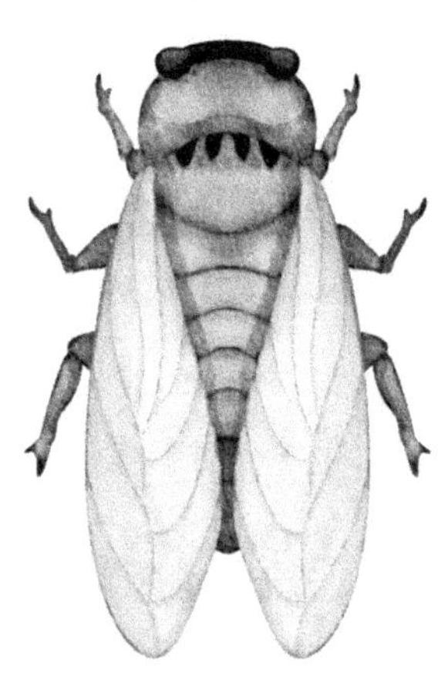

Cicadas are fascinating insects with a life cycle that is as intricate as it is unique. Understanding their life cycle is crucial to appreciating the significance of their periodic emergences. This chapter delves into the different stages of a cicada's life, from egg to nymph to adult, shedding light on the remarkable journey these insects undertake.

Egg Stage: The Beginning of Life:

The life cycle of a cicada begins when a female cicada lays her eggs. Female cicadas use their ovipositors, specialized egg-laying structures, to insert eggs into the twigs and branches of trees. A single female can lay hundreds of eggs in multiple locations, ensuring the propagation of the species. Eggs are typically laid in tree branches, with each female capable of laying up to 400 eggs. These eggs hatch in six to ten weeks, marking the start of the cicada's life.

Nymph Stage: Life Underground:

Once the eggs hatch, tiny nymphs resembling miniature adults fall to the ground and immediately burrow into the soil, where they will spend most of their lives. This stage, characterized by slow growth and development over several years, is crucial for their survival and maturation.

Cicada nymphs are uniquely adapted for their subterranean habitat. Their forelegs are strong digging tools, enabling efficient tunneling through the soil. They attach themselves to tree roots, using specialized mouthparts to extract nutrient-rich xylem sap, which sustains them throughout their long developmental period.

Emergence: The Transition to Adulthood:

After spending years underground, cicada nymphs are finally ready to emerge. Triggered by temperature and internal cues, they dig their way to the surface, typically at night. This synchronized event sees millions of cicadas emerging simultaneously. Emergence usually occurs in late spring or early summer, marking a dramatic transformation in the cicadas' life cycle.

The nymphs climb trees and other vertical surfaces to molt. This process, called ecdysis, involves shedding their exoskeletons to transition into winged adults. The transformation is a vulnerable time for cicadas, as they are soft and pale immediately after molting, making them easy targets for predators. Within a few hours, their bodies harden, and their colors darken, preparing them for life above ground.

Adult Stage: The Finale:

Once they have molted, cicadas enter their adult stage, which lasts only a few weeks. During this brief period, adult cicadas focus on mating and laying the next generation of eggs. Male cicadas are known for their loud calls, used to attract females. These calls can reach up to 100 decibels, making them one of the loudest insects in the world.

After mating, females lay their eggs in the branches of trees, using their ovipositors to make slits in the bark. Each female can lay hundreds of eggs, ensuring the continuation of the species. The adult cicadas' life above ground is short-lived, typically lasting about four to six weeks. After completing their reproductive mission, adult cicadas die, and the cycle begins anew.

A detailed close-up photograph of a cicada, highlighting its intricate features such as the wings, eyes, and body.

Fun Facts:

-Cicadas have the longest life cycle of any insect, with some species spending up to 17 years underground.

-The sound of a cicada's call can reach 100 decibels, equivalent to the noise of a motorcycle.

-Despite their noisy presence, cicadas do not bite or sting and are harmless to humans.

Understanding the life cycle of cicadas not only enhances our appreciation for these remarkable insects but also underscores the importance of preserving their habitats. As we delve deeper into their world, we uncover the intricate balance of nature that supports their existence and, by extension, the health of our ecosystems.

Interactive Element:

Activity:

Create a Cicada Life Cycle Wheel: Using paper and markers, create a wheel that illustrates each stage of the cicada life cycle. This hands-on activity helps reinforce the concepts learned in this chapter and provides a visual aid for understanding the progression from egg to adult.

CHAPTER 2: THE ECOLOGICAL ROLE OF CICADAS

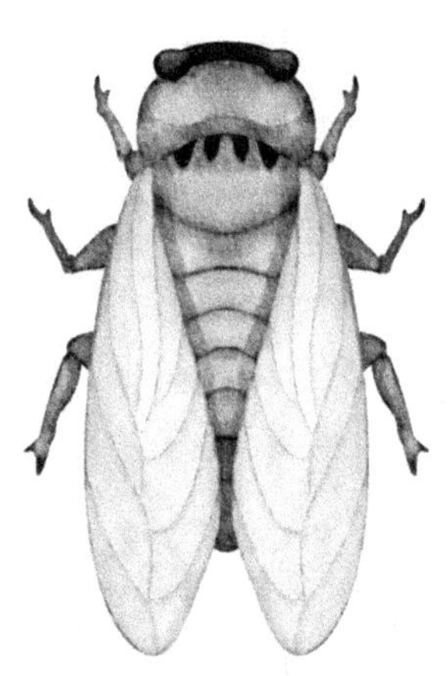

Cicadas are more than just noisy insects that appear every few years; they play a crucial role in maintaining the balance of our ecosystems. This chapter explores the various ecological contributions of cicadas, from nutrient cycling to soil aeration, and highlights their importance in the natural world.

Nutrient Cycling:

One of the most significant ecological contributions of cicadas is their role in nutrient cycling. When cicadas emerge en masse and subsequently die, their bodies decompose and release valuable nutrients back into the soil. This process enriches the soil and supports plant growth by enhancing soil fertility, benefiting plants and trees, and leading to increased plant growth and productivity.

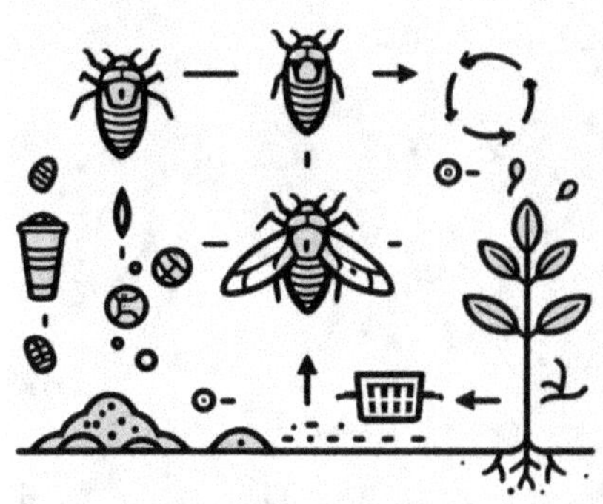

Food Source:

Cicadas provide a substantial food source for a variety of predators, making them a critical component of the food web in their habitats. Birds, mammals, reptiles, and even other insects eagerly consume cicadas during their emergence periods. This abundance of cicadas offers a significant nutritional boost to these predators, often leading to increased breeding success and higher survival rates for their offspring.

The sudden influx of cicadas can significantly impact the population dynamics of their predators. This phenomenon, known as "predator satiation," occurs when the sheer number of cicadas overwhelms predators, allowing many cicadas to escape predation and reproduce. This strategy ensures the survival of the species despite heavy predation, illustrating the intricate balance within ecosystems where cicadas play a vital role.

Soil Aeration:

The activities of cicada nymphs underground play a vital role in soil aeration. As nymphs burrow and move through the soil, they create tunnels that allow air and water to penetrate deeper into the ground, improving soil health. These tunnels help to loosen the soil, promoting root growth and enhancing water infiltration, which supports healthier plant growth. The extensive network of tunnels left behind by cicadas continues to benefit soil structure long after the nymphs have emerged and molted.

Tree Pruning:

Cicada egg-laying behavior can act as a natural pruning mechanism for trees. When female cicadas lay their eggs in tree branches, it often causes the branches to die and fall off. This natural pruning can stimulate new growth and improve the overall health of the tree. By reducing overcrowding in the tree canopy, this process can lead to increased sunlight penetration and air circulation, further benefiting the tree's health. This unintended pruning effect can contribute to the overall vigor and longevity of the trees, demonstrating yet another way cicadas impact their environment.

Soil Aeration:

 The activities of cicada nymphs underground play a vital role in soil aeration. As nymphs burrow and move through the soil, they create tunnels that allow air and water to penetrate deeper into the ground, improving soil health.

Key Points:
-Burrowing nymphs create a network of tunnels that aerate the soil.
-Improved soil aeration promotes root growth and water infiltration.
-Aerated soil supports healthier plant growth.

Tree Pruning:

 Cicada egg-laying behavior can act as a natural pruning mechanism for trees. When female cicadas lay their eggs in tree branches, it often causes the branches to die and fall off. This natural pruning can stimulate new growth and improve the overall health of the tree.

Key Points:
-Female cicadas lay eggs in small branches, causing them to die and break off.
-This natural pruning can promote new growth and reduce overcrowding in the tree canopy.
-Pruned trees often show increased vigor and health.

Fun Facts:

-Cicada emergences are so significant that they can influence the behavior and population dynamics of their predators.

-The tunnels created by cicada nymphs can remain in the soil long after the nymphs have emerged, continuing to benefit soil aeration for years.

-Cicadas have a symbiotic relationship with certain fungi, which help them break down tough plant material in their diet.

Understanding the ecological role of cicadas helps us appreciate their importance beyond their seasonal appearances. These insects contribute to the health and balance of ecosystems in ways that might not be immediately obvious but are crucial for maintaining the natural world.

CHAPTER 3: THE GREAT CICADA EMERGENCE OF 2024 IN THE USA

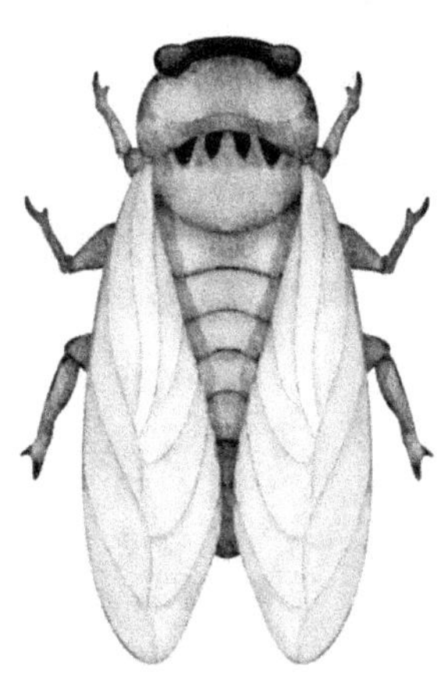

The 2024 cicada emergence is set to be one of the most spectacular natural events in recent history. This chapter delves into what makes the 2024 emergence unique, the geographic locations most affected, and the impact on daily life, media coverage, and scientific studies.

Overview of the 2024 Emergence:

Every 13 to 17 years, billions of cicadas emerge from the ground in a synchronized event that captivates scientists and the public alike. The 2024 emergence is expected to be particularly noteworthy due to the large brood set to appear. Broods XIII and X are anticipated to surface, bringing an unprecedented scale of emergence. This event provides valuable insights into cicada behavior and their interactions with the environment.

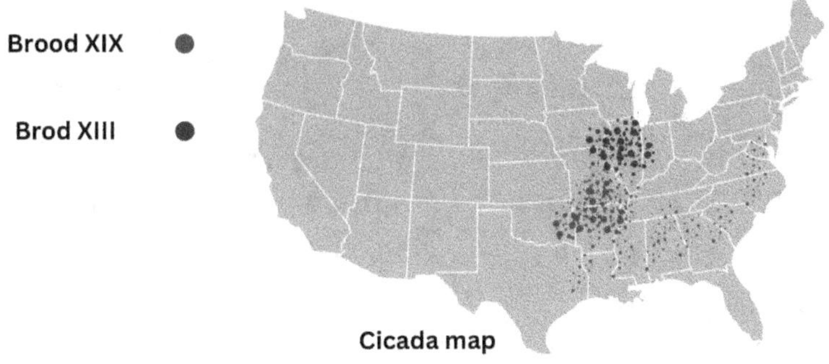

Cicada map

Geographic Locations:

 The 2024 cicada emergence will predominantly affect the eastern United States, with significant activity in states like Ohio, Indiana, Illinois, and Pennsylvania. These areas will host the largest concentrations of Brood XIII and Brood X cicadas, leading to a dramatic and widespread event. The emergence will vary slightly in timing across different regions, typically beginning in late spring and continuing into early summer.

In Ohio, cities such as Cincinnati, Columbus, and Cleveland will experience high cicada activity. Residents can expect to see cicadas emerging from the ground in large numbers, filling the air with their distinctive calls. Parks, wooded areas, and suburban neighborhoods with mature trees will be prime locations for witnessing this phenomenon.

Indiana will also see a substantial emergence, particularly in the southern and central parts of the state. Areas around Indianapolis and Bloomington are expected to have dense cicada populations. The presence of Brood XIII and Brood X will make this event especially notable, drawing attention from scientists and enthusiasts alike.

Illinois, especially the central and northern regions, will be another hotspot for cicada activity. Cities like Springfield, Peoria, and the outskirts of Chicago will experience significant emergences. The cicadas' presence will be felt in both urban and rural settings, offering a unique opportunity for widespread observation and study.

Pennsylvania, known for its diverse landscapes and rich biodiversity, will also host a large number of cicadas. Regions around Pittsburgh, Harrisburg, and Philadelphia will be buzzing with cicada activity. The state's numerous parks and natural reserves will provide excellent vantage points for observing the emergence.

These geographic variations in cicada emergence highlight the broad impact of this natural event across multiple states. Each region's unique environment will influence the behavior and distribution of cicadas, providing diverse opportunities for observation and study. Understanding these geographic differences is crucial for appreciating the full scope of the 2024 cicada emergence.

Impact on Daily Life:

The sudden influx of cicadas can have various effects on daily life, from the incessant sound of their calls to the influence on local wildlife and human activities. While some people might find the presence of cicadas overwhelming, others see it as a unique opportunity to engage with nature. Outdoor activities and events might need adjustments, but the chance to observe such a massive natural phenomenon is unmatched.

Media Coverage and Public Reaction:

Media outlets across the country will likely cover the cicada emergence extensively, highlighting both the scientific significance and public fascination. Social media will also play a crucial role in sharing experiences and observations. Public engagement through citizen science projects will allow individuals to contribute to ongoing research, making this a participatory event.

Scientific Studies and Findings:

The 2024 emergence presents a valuable opportunity for scientists to study cicadas in greater detail. Ongoing research will focus on various aspects of cicada biology, behavior, and ecology. Key scientific questions include understanding their life cycle, mating behaviors, and their impact on the environment. The public can contribute to these studies by participating in observation and data collection efforts.

Timing of the Emergence:

The 2024 cicada emergence is expected to begin in late spring, typically around mid-May, and continue into early summer. The exact timing can vary slightly depending on local temperatures and soil conditions, but the peak activity usually occurs over a few weeks during this period.

Interactive Element:

Activity:

Capture the 2024 cicada emergence through photography: Over the course of the emergence period, take five unique photographs of cicadas. These photos can include cicadas emerging from the ground, on tree bark, their molted exoskeletons, interactions with predators, or any other interesting cicada-related scenes you encounter.

Share Your Work:

 Create a photo album or share your best shots on social media with the hashtag #Cicada2024Darcy. Consider participating in local or online photo contests focused on this natural event.

CHAPTER 4: HOW TO OBSERVE AND APPRECIATE THE 2024 CICADA EMERGENCE

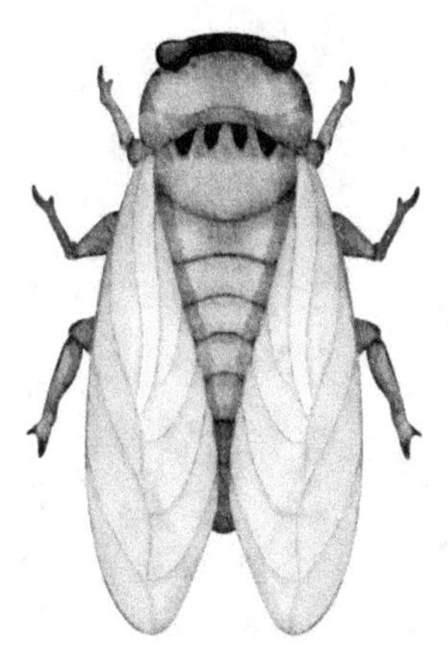

Observing the cicada emergence is a unique and rewarding experience. This chapter provides practical tips and advice on how to make the most of this natural event, including where and when to watch, what to look for, and how to contribute to citizen science projects.

Best Times and Locations for Observation:

Cicadas are most active during the early morning and late afternoon. Knowing where to go and when to be there is key to a successful observation experience. Ideal locations include forested areas and parks in regions with high cicada activity, such as Ohio, Indiana, Illinois, and Pennsylvania.

What to Look For:

During the cicada emergence, there are several fascinating behaviors and phenomena to observe:

Nymphs Emerging from the Ground: Look for small holes in the ground, which indicate where nymphs are emerging. You may also see the nymphs climbing tree trunks or other vertical surfaces.

Molting Process: Observe the transformation as nymphs shed their exoskeletons to become winged adults. This process, called ecdysis, can often be seen on tree bark or leaves.

Adult Cicadas: Once they have molted, adult cicadas can be seen resting on trees and shrubs. Their distinctive wings and large, red eyes make them easy to spot.

Mating Calls: Listen for the loud, distinctive calls of male cicadas as they try to attract females. The chorus of cicada calls can be deafening at times, creating a unique soundscape.

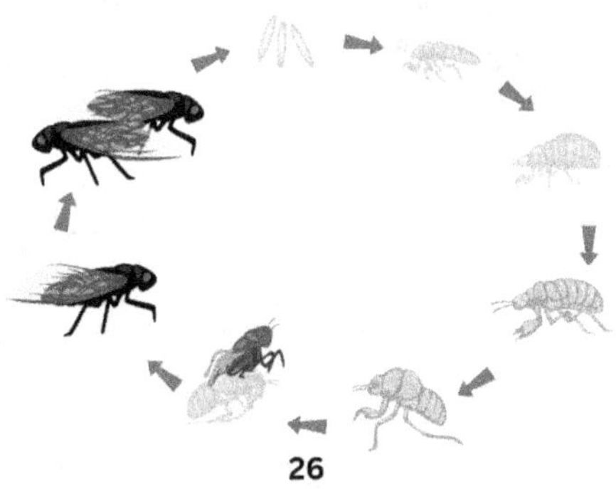

Tips for Safe and Respectful Observation:

Respecting the natural environment and ensuring your safety is crucial when observing cicadas. Interact with the habitat responsibly by avoiding unnecessary disturbances. Bring essentials like water, sunscreen, and insect repellent to ensure a comfortable experience.

Interactive Element:

Activity:

Cicada Observation Journal: Start a journal where you can record your observations of cicadas. Note where and when you see them, their behavior, and any interactions with other animals. This activity helps you engage with the natural world and understand the role of cicadas in your local ecosystem.

CHAPTER 5: CICADA MYTHS AND LEGENDS

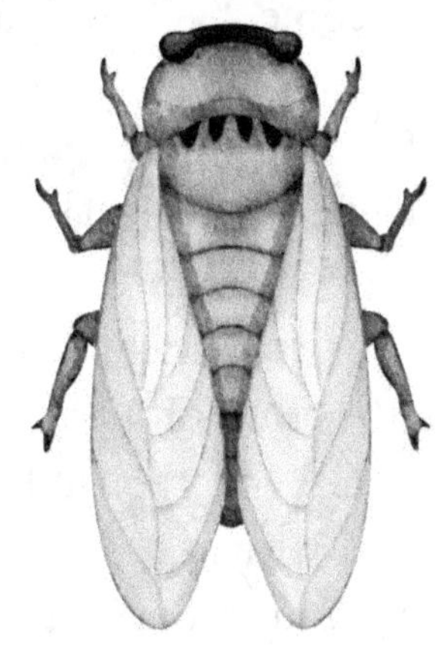

Cicadas have fascinated humans for millennia, inspiring a wealth of myths, legends, and superstitions across different cultures. This chapter explores some of the most intriguing stories and beliefs about cicadas, highlighting their cultural significance and the various ways they have been perceived throughout history.

Ancient Greece: The Symbol of Rebirth and Immortality:

In ancient Greece, cicadas were associated with rebirth and immortality. The Greeks admired cicadas for their ability to seemingly come back to life after spending years underground. The poet Anacreon praised the cicada for its carefree life and immortality, as it was believed to live on dew and never die.

Myth of Tithonus: One of the most famous Greek myths involving cicadas is the story of Tithonus, a mortal who was granted immortality by the gods but not eternal youth. As he aged and withered, he transformed into a cicada, eternally singing his mournful song.

An ancient Greek vase depicting cicadas.

Chinese Culture: The Symbol of Resurrection and Nobility:

In Chinese culture, cicadas are symbols of resurrection and nobility. The ancient Chinese regarded cicadas as noble creatures because of their pure diet of plant sap and their life cycle, which mirrors the cycle of death and rebirth.

Funerary Practices: Jade cicadas were often placed in the mouths of the deceased to ensure the soul's safe passage to the afterlife and to symbolize the hope of resurrection.

Poetry and Literature: Cicadas often appear in Chinese poetry, symbolizing the transient nature of life and the purity of spirit.

Photograph of a jade cicada used in ancient Chinese burials.

Japanese Culture: The Harbinger of Summer and Ephemeral Beauty:

In Japan, cicadas are seen as harbingers of summer and symbols of the fleeting nature of life. Their brief but intense period of activity above ground resonates with the Japanese appreciation for the ephemeral beauty of life, akin to the cherry blossom.

Haiku and Literature: Cicadas frequently appear in Japanese haiku and literature, symbolizing both the joys and the transience of life. The sound of cicadas is a common motif in Japanese poetry, evoking the heat of summer and the passage of time.

Cicada Symbolism: In Japanese culture, cicadas are also symbols of reincarnation and the impermanence of life, reflecting Buddhist influences.

Traditional Japanese haiku featuring cicadas, with a background of cicada illustrations.

Native American Legends: The Trickster and Transformer:

Many Native American tribes have their own stories and legends about cicadas. In some traditions, cicadas are seen as tricksters or transformers, capable of changing their form or outsmarting other creatures.

Hopi Legend: In Hopi mythology, cicadas are associated with the Katsina, spiritual beings that bring rain and fertility. Cicada Katsina are believed to play a role in the regeneration of the land.

Cicada Songs: Some Native American tribes use cicada songs in their rituals, believing the sounds to be a call for rain or a signal of changing seasons.

Illustration of a cicada Katsina doll used in Hopi rituals.

African Folklore: The Messenger of the Ancestors:

In various African cultures, cicadas are considered messengers of the ancestors. Their songs are thought to carry messages from the spirit world to the living.

Zulu Beliefs: Among the Zulu, cicadas are believed to have a connection to the ancestors, and their appearance and singing are seen as signs of ancestral communication and guidance.

Cicada in African Proverbs: Cicadas often appear in African proverbs and stories, symbolizing resilience, persistence, and the cycle of life.

Traditional African artwork featuring cicadas.

European Superstitions:

Omens and Symbols of Luck: In Europe, cicadas have been both revered and feared. They are often seen as omens, either of good luck or impending misfortune.

French Tradition: In Provence, France, cicadas are celebrated as symbols of good luck and prosperity. Ceramic cicadas are often used as decorations to bring good fortune to homes.

Cicada in Literature: European literature, especially in the Romantic period, often featured cicadas as symbols of nature's beauty and the inexorable passage of time.

Photograph of a ceramic cicada from Provence, France.

Modern Interpretations:

Pop Culture and Beyond: Cicadas continue to capture the human imagination in modern times, appearing in various forms of pop culture, from music and literature to movies and video games.

Literature and Film: Cicadas often symbolize the passage of time and the cyclical nature of life in contemporary literature and film. Their distinctive song is used to evoke a sense of summer, nostalgia, or even foreboding.

Music and Art: Cicadas have inspired musicians and artists, symbolizing themes of transformation, persistence, and the beauty of nature.

A collage of cicada representations in music, literature, and film.

Interactive Element: Cicada Storytelling Challenge:

Activity:
Write your own myth or legend involving cicadas. Use elements from different cultures or create an entirely new story.

Final Thoughts:

Cicadas have left an indelible mark on human culture, inspiring stories, songs, and symbols that resonate with the cycles of nature and life. By exploring these myths and legends, we gain a deeper appreciation for these remarkable insects and their place in our collective imagination.

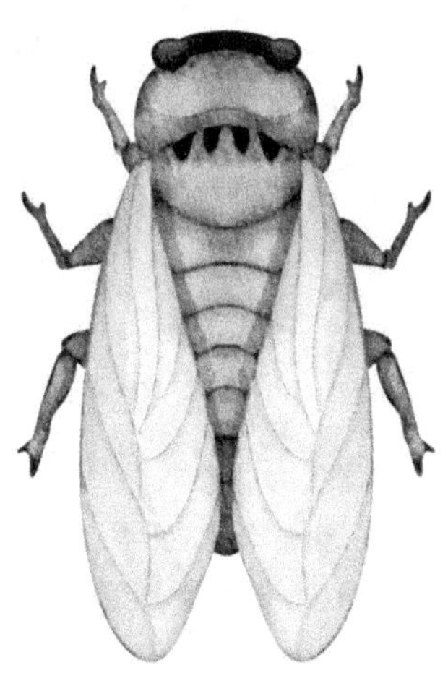

CONCLUSION

As we draw to the end of "Cicada Chronicles: The 2024 Emergence," it's clear that cicadas are more than just noisy insects—they are remarkable creatures with a profound impact on our environment, culture, and science. This book has taken you through their intricate life cycle, highlighted their ecological roles, and celebrated their rich presence in myths and legends across the world.

The 2024 emergence is a rare and spectacular event that provides a unique opportunity to witness nature's wonders firsthand. Whether you are a curious observer, a dedicated scientist, or simply someone who appreciates the rhythms of nature, the cicadas' synchronized emergence is a reminder of the intricate and interconnected web of life.

Through our journey, we have explored how cicadas contribute to soil aeration, natural tree pruning, and serve as a critical food source for many animals. Their life cycle, spent mostly underground before a brief, dazzling appearance above ground, underscores the themes of transformation and renewal.

Cicadas have inspired countless myths and legends, symbolizing rebirth, immortality, and the fleeting nature of life. From ancient Greece to modern Japan, these insects have been revered and incorporated into the cultural fabric of societies around the globe.

As we prepare for the 2024 emergence, let us embrace this event with wonder and respect. Participate in citizen science projects, observe responsibly, and contribute to conservation efforts to ensure that future generations can also experience the magic of cicada emergences.

In closing, cicadas remind us of the beauty and complexity of the natural world. Their song, a chorus of survival and continuity, invites us to pause and listen, to reflect on our place within the ecosystem, and to marvel at the cycles of life that continue around us.

Thank you for joining this exploration of cicadas. May your encounters with these fascinating insects inspire awe, curiosity, and a deeper connection to nature.

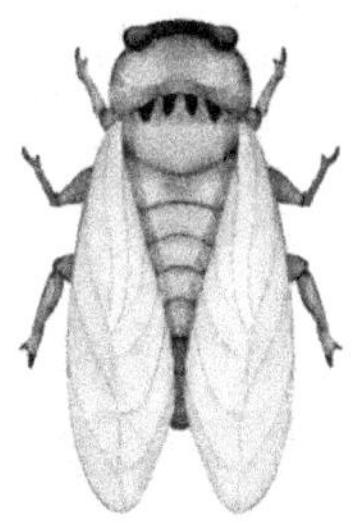

BIBLIOGRAPHY

"Cicadas!" by Laurence Pringle
Publication Date: March 1, 2010
Edition: 1st Edition
A comprehensive book covering the life cycle, behavior, and significance of cicadas.

"Periodical Cicadas: The Brood X Edition" by Gene Kritsky
Publication Date: May 1, 2021
Edition: Updated Edition
Delves into the history and science of Brood X, one of the most studied cicada broods.

"Cicadas: What They Are, Where They Live, and Their Life Cycle" by Margaret Hall
Publication Date: September 1, 2009
Edition: 1st Edition
Provides useful information about cicadas, their habitats, and their life cycles.

"Searching For Cicadas" by Lesley Gibbes and Judy Watson
Publication Date: June 1, 2020
Edition: 1st Edition
A beautifully illustrated book capturing the adventure of discovering cicadas.

"Cicadas (True Books)" by Ann O. Squire
Publication Date: March 1, 2010
Edition: 1st Edition
Offers a clear and engaging overview of cicadas.

"The Cicadas are Coming" by Doug Wechsler
Publication Date: April 15, 2021
Edition: 1st Edition
Focuses on the 17-year cicadas with high-quality photographs.

"What to Expect When You're Expecting... Cicadas!" by Dr. Martha Weiss
Publication Date: May 1, 2021
Edition: 1st Edition
An informative book with high-quality illustrations explaining cicadas' lifecycle and emergence.

"Cecily Cicada" by Doug Wechsler
Publication Date: April 1, 2005
Edition: 1st Edition
A rhyming book following the journey of a cicada.

"Cicadas don't bug me" by Doug Wechsler
Publication Date: May 15, 2011
Edition: 1st Edition
Introduces young students to cicadas in a fun and engaging way.